Other books by Judith L. Pearson

*Belly of the Beast*

*The Wolves at the Door*

# IT'S JUST HAIR

## 20 Essential Life Lessons

Judith L. Pearson

Courage Concepts
PUBLISHING

www.courageconceptspublishing.com

*It's Just Hair: 20 Essential Life Lessons*

Requests for information and permission should be addressed to
Courage Concepts Publishing,
www.courageconceptspublishing.com
*info@courageconcepts.com*

Cover design by
Genevieve Margherio

ISBN 978-0-9850929-0-0

To order additional copies, or to buy books in quantity, please visit
www.courageconceptspublishing.com
or email: info@courageconcepts.com

*If you're going through hell, keep going.*
- Winston Churchill

## Acknowledgements:

People sometimes skip the acknowledgments in books. Not me. I think they tell a lot about the author and give you great insight into what the rest of the book will be like. To those of you reading these words then, I hope neither I nor the book disappoints.

If it were not for the skills of my doctors and nurses, I wouldn't be around to write at all. Kudos then to Dr. Nancy Kalinowsky, Dr. Marcia Liepman, Dr. Michael Nave and the staffs of the infusions centers at Allegan General Hospital and South Haven Community Hospital for my care, as well as for all you do toward the betterment of medicine.

Thanks to the hard work of my editors: Amber Essex, Elaine Fluck, Anne Habicht, Mary McCallum, Elizabeth Schmitt, Lisa Schmitt, Danielle Streed and Pat Thomas. Not only did your eagle eyes and quick minds make this a better book, but we all remained friends in the process.

My sons Nick and Sean never failed to make me laugh, make me think, or give me a push when I needed it. Thank you for being the men you are.

The encouragement of my friends and extended family has been invaluable, not only toward good health but also in putting this project together. Whenever you need me, I've got your backs.

Lastly, this writer is without words when it comes to thanking her husband. We had only been married 10 months when cancer came to call. It was certainly not what you had signed up for, darling David, but your humor and strength filled in perfectly when mine failed. Happily, this saga has made our love an unbreakable bond.

# Introduction

*Diseases can be our spiritual flat tires - disruptions in
our lives that seem to be disasters at the time
but end by redirecting our lives in a meaningful way.*
- Bernie S. Siegel

I can't tell you how other people react when
they're told they have cancer. I can only tell you how I
reacted. I became two people: the me who had breast
cancer, and the me who watched the me who had breast
cancer. The Cancer Me dutifully reported for dozens of
doctors' appointments, scans and tests. The Watcher Me
would observe the events and ask the Cancer Me
questions, taking careful notes. The result is the book
you are now holding.

By design, we are never given much preparation
for things as life-altering as a diagnosis of cancer. If we

knew in advance how badly we would feel about it, we'd spend all of our healthy days worrying about what dire diagnoses might be hanging in our futures. That doesn't even take into consideration all of the other dark possibilities lurking: car accidents, job loss, divorce. It's just too awful to imagine. So we don't.

In 2011, my focus was on my eldest son, stationed in England with his wife and their two children. He was about to be deployed to the war in Afghanistan, and to send him off properly, my younger son and his sweetheart, and my husband and I had planned a grand get-together at their home in Britain. My cancer diagnosis came six weeks before the trip. Fate has a funny way of derailing plans, doesn't it?

I hold three beliefs, however, that I would not allow to be derailed. First, the Cancer Me would never define who I was as a person. She was only going to be a tiny part of who I am, like a few grains of sand on a wide expanse of beach. Secondly, everything happens for a reason, even bad things. The tricky part is figuring out the message. Finally, we must all serve humanity in some way. The size of that service is not important; but it's really cool if our adversity can become a stepping stone for someone else.

With those beliefs in mind, after all was said and done, I examined my journey for ways it had changed my life for the better. In so doing, I realized that every step I had taken was a metaphor for the steps we all take in life. If I removed the words cancer and all others associated with it, the lessons I learned would fit any of life's challenges.

Was this journey difficult? You bet. Do others have it worse? You bet. Has this journey changed me? You bet.

My husband told me soon after my diagnosis that I was going to have the unique opportunity to live out in real life the last scene from the movie *It's a Wonderful Life*. Jimmy Stewart's character, George Bailey, in the midst of feeling as though he's worthless, realizes how much impact he's had on the lives of others. And they, in turn, come to his aide when he needs them the most.

The love and prayers of my family and friends helped me learn these lessons. My duty now is to pay it forward; to share the feelings of the Cancer Me and the meandering notes of the Watcher Me with others, in the hope that they might see through the darkness, and just as George Bailey did, realize that their lives can be pretty wonderful too.

# Lesson 1:

# You Were Chosen

*We could never learn to be brave and patient
if there were only joy in the world.*
- Helen Keller


"Red Rover, Red Rover, send Judy right over!"
Remember that game?  Two teams locked arms and took
turns calling out members from the opposing team.
When your name was called, you ran at the other guys
with the goal of breaking through their line.  If you did,
you took someone back to your team with you.  If you
failed, you became part of the opposing team. In a
defensive maneuver teams called the really good players
from the opposing line early on, figuring their team was
at its strongest since it still had a full complement of

participants. If the good players failed to break the line, they had to stay, thereby strengthening the team. Everyone knew this strategy. Consequently, your social status rose commensurately the earlier you were chosen. It meant you were a skilled Red Rover player, and that made your playground future look brighter.

Now that we're all grown up, it's still prestigious to be a member of the chosen few: promoted to the best positions at work, invited to join the coolest organizations, even coupled with the most desirable member of the opposite sex. We're familiar with those sought-after accolades. But did you know we've all been chosen for other, less recognized, but no less important, appointments as well?

READER ALERT: Here comes a statement that may cause you to think I've lost my mind.
I haven't. Bear with me.

Many people might say that I fell victim to breast cancer. To that I would resolutely and firmly proclaim I am NOT a victim. I was CHOSEN to have breast cancer, along with 288,000 other women in 2011, a number that climbs every year. We're chosen because our experiences can help myriad others in the future, both through our own works as well as the work of our doctors as they treat us. What a humbling opportunity for us to help others in need!

And being chosen is certainly not limited to just breast cancer. The group includes those suffering from other diseases, those who've lost their jobs, those who suddenly find themselves single through death or divorce, those with difficult children. The list is comprised of those with any issue that stops them in their tracks. In other words, EVERYONE is chosen some time.

I'll grant you it takes courage to look at your misfortune and call yourself chosen. But here are five intriguing reasons to do so:

1.  **"No woman is an island."** Okay, John Donne really said no man, but gender doesn't matter. What does matter is that we're all interconnected. We've learned all we know from other people, whether they're in our sphere of influence or not. Helping one another is what makes us a community of happy humans.

2. **You, too, can be a research rat.** Even if you don't lift a finger, the experience for which you were chosen can aid doctors, scientists, researchers, social psychologists, your friends and family, and more, so that others might avoid what's challenging you now. Or at least they could have an easier ride.

3. **Give 'em a break.** Those who love us feel nearly as bad as we do about the situation for which we've been chosen. However, if *we* look at it as an opportunity to aid society, our support group might as well, and that will take some of the burden off of them.

4. **Champion role model.** Finding good role models for our kids among headline-makers is tough, but who needs them when *we've* been chosen! When the kids in your life see you standing up to adversity, it will make it easier for them to do the same thing when they're chosen. (Remember, whether we like it or not, everyone is chosen for something. And they will be too.)

5. **Like lima beans, it's good for YOU!** If those four reasons don't float your boat, this one surely will. Having the attitude that you were chosen for

your challenge should make you feel special. You wouldn't have been chosen if some good couldn't come from it. Furthermore, this attitude gets your mind off you. Finally, facing down something you've been chosen for might just allow you to take on new challenges with even more robust courage.

Bottom line, it doesn't matter whether what you've been chosen for helps one person or one million. What counts is that you held out your hand and shared your experiences. After all, you were chosen to do so.

# Lesson 2:

# Here Be Dragons

*The world is round and the place which may seem like the end may also be the beginning.*
- Ivy Baker Priest

Once upon a time all the smartest people in the world thought the earth was flat, that it was actually a disk, bobbing like a log in the vast ocean. Since they weren't sure of what might exist in the ocean beyond their comfortable disk, these smart people took a better-safe-than-sorry approach. They cautioned against the dangers beyond their known world, speaking of "dog-headed beings," and warning, "Here also are huge men having horns four feet long, and there are serpents of such magnitude that they can eat an ox whole." Ancient maps went further still, featuring drawings of monsters living in a dark ocean. One map took the notion to the extreme, inscribed with the words: "Here be dragons."

We're now secure in the knowledge that we're not living on some kind of floating saucer and that there aren't monsters waiting to gobble us up if we fall off the edge. Some historians have even suggested that what might have looked and behaved like dragons, when seen by early mariners, were actually"algae-impregnated icebergs," no more capable of eating them alive than an ice cube in a modern day gin and tonic.

Actually, what early civilizations feared still terrifies us today. It's the oldest bogeyman of them all: the unknown. Children, surrounded by modern technology, still fear what's in the closet or under the bed at night. They've never seen anything scary there, and have most probably never been given reason to be afraid. It's what *might* be lurking there that's so frightening.

One of the most powerful childhood threats, a true journey into the unknown, came in the form of these words: "This is going on your permanent record!" It was voiced by parents, teachers and scout leaders alike, and it was rarely said in a positive light. It brings up questions. Where *is* my permanent record? Is it still being added to? And when does someone actually review it? I don't think anyone's mentioned it to me since high school graduation, but for the first 18 years of my life, its significance, an unknown, terrified me.

We always assume what we don't know or don't understand will hurt us. When we're faced with life challenges, the outcomes of which we're uncertain, our ancient brains instinctively steer us toward fear. A diagnosis, a lost job, the departure of a spouse; a unknown or unfamiliar scenario can make our lives stretch out after it like a big, dark ocean. It's overwhelming and very frightening.

But it doesn't have to be that way. There's an old joke that goes like this: How do you eat an elephant? The answer: One bite at a time. As a joke, it's not so great. But as an ideology it's pretty darn good. We may not be able to take on the whole ocean, but we *are* capable of taking on a glass or two of water each day. That means

Mom,

First, let me say that I am proud of how well you are taking this. I know it must be a very stressful time for you, and you are definitely in my prayers. Amber asked me a few weeks ago what I thought she should do if someone tried to break into the house. After a few moments of thought, I told her that attitude played a huge part in not only operating around threats in the deployed theater, but also in day-to-day life. I told her that after dealing with the all the bad seeds I've seen in my career, you have to own your space and basically tell them where to go, because you're the only bad ass in town. I have read and been instructed on countless studies that focused on injured police officers' and soldiers' attitudes after they were attacked. The study showed that those officers and soldiers who had a "never give up" attitude survived their injuries and were even able to counter attack. This was based against those officers and soldiers who notoriously had poor attitudes and were not in shape, and who eventually fell victim to far less serious injuries. What am I trying to say? Well, it is definitely not our family's way to roll over when the going gets tough. So I say you stay prepared by keeping healthy and having a plan to deal with the worst. And more importantly, if it is the worst, you say, "I'm the only bad ass in town," and you make it pay for ruining your day. I love you with all my heart.

Two weeks later, he shared yet another lesson with me.

Mom,

I wanted to give you a little reminder just in case you needed a good swift kick in the pants. Amber told me that you have not been eating very much. I remember the academy harped on staying fit because you never know when you will be fighting for your life. I have tried to take that to heart. I know I eat better than I used to, and I definitely work out 500% more than I did before. I plan on hitting it extra hard in the next months before I deploy.

What I am trying to say is you need to make sure you've got everything in order, because you are going to war as well. Even though it is a little different than the war I am used to, I would say it is far more important. I know it's hard to find the time, but you need to push the stress aside, stay active and eat well. I believe it will make the fight, and your recovery, that much easier. I know you know everything I have mentioned in this email, but I wanted to give you a simple reminder. I think through all of this I have found my place. I have no doubt that most of the friends and family who call you cry and tell you how sorry they are. Well, I am not that kind of person. You need to tackle this head on and not get complacent. I love

you very much and any time you need to get
toughened up a little, give me a call.

These words, written with a great deal of love and sincerity, reminded me that help often comes from unexpected corners of our lives. While I'm quite sure my disease was the biggest shock either of my sons had ever received - made more difficult by the fact that both live thousands of miles away from me, in opposite directions - each played a critical role in my recovery. All the drama involved in child rearing, the sleepless nights and the days I just wanted to call it quits, was obviously worth the effort.

# Lesson 4:

# Inside-Out

*Everything has beauty; but not everyone sees it.*
- Confucius

The day I went to meet my surgeon for the first time was a big deal. In that woman's hands would rest my future, not only in terms of removing the cancer, but also in terms of what my body would ultimately look like. I fretted over what to wear. I wanted to look secure in my appearance, but vulnerable enough so she'd want to take good care of me; courageous, but not as though I didn't care; cancerous, but otherwise healthy.

I was very chatty during the 45 minute car trip to her office. I repeated to my husband that I was okay if she felt the best solution to the whole mess was a mastectomy rather than a lumpectomy. Hell, I told him, she can take 'em both if she thinks it's best. Clearly, it was a premature burst of bravado.

My surgeon was encouraging. Based on the diagnostics taken thus far, she believed the cancer was contained to just my left breast. According to the scans, she had identified two satellite tumors orbiting the mother ship, the tumor I had found. Consequently, she was going to have to remove a great deal of tissue, and therefore recommended a mastectomy.

MASTECTOMY. The word makes a woman's blood run cold. All that bravado I had in me during the car ride to the surgeon's office? Gone, blown right out window on a spring breeze. The first ten minutes or so of the ride home were pretty quiet. When I could finally move my jaws, I voiced my greatest concern. "I'm not going to be the same woman you married a year ago. I'm going to look very different."

In retrospect, it was a ridiculous statement. I had just been told my cancer hadn't spread. I wonder, on any given day, how many thousands of people wish they could receive that message? And yet all I was worried about was, at the end of it all, how I was going to look. My husband proceeded to teach me a very important lesson.

"There are some people," he said, "who are beautiful on the outside but have nothing on the inside. They're outside-in people. There are others who are beautiful on the inside and it radiates to the outside, regardless of other circumstances. They're inside-out people, and they're always beautiful. You are one of those."

He followed up with all the wonderful things a woman wants her husband to say, under any circumstances, but in the days that followed, I mulled this over very carefully.

In the spring of 1962, *Vogue Magazine* coined the phrase "beautiful people." At the time it referred to then First Lady Jacqueline Kennedy and all of the glamor that surrounded life in the Kennedy White House. While we may not utter the phrase as often now, everyone still knows who the beautiful people are. By journalistic standards they are those who are well-dressed, well-coiffed, and look as though they don't have a care in the world. They appear in exotic locales, at dazzling events, and always with other beautiful people in tow. Many of us, at one time or another, have dreamt about life as one of the beautiful people, those referred to by my husband as the outside-in people. What a terrible waste of a dream.

The people we should really emulate are the inside-out people. We may not notice them right away. They're the ones who speak quietly, but love largely. They're the ones who always have enough time, if not enough money. They're the ones who give all of the credit to others, never considering keeping any of it for themselves. They don't have lavish homes, big jewelry, or entourages. Instead their names are mostly unknown and their works often go unnoticed until they're gone.

It takes a lot of courage to be an inside-out person. How many can you think of? Find them, thank them, mimic them. Then imagine how wonderful a world full of inside-out people, and those who love them, would be.

# Lesson 5:

# It's Just Hair

*If I had my life to live over, I would perhaps have more
actual troubles, but I'd have fewer imaginary ones.*
- Don Herold

Fact: The fastest car in the world is the Bugatti Veyron
Super Sport; zero to 60 in 2.4 seconds, top speed,
267 miles per hour.  Base price: $2.4 million.

Fact: The largest home in America is the Biltmore Estate
in Asheville, N.C.; 250 rooms, 43 bathrooms,
175,000 square feet.  Estimated worth: $2.5 - $3
billion.

Fact: Americans spend more on hair care products and
services than on any other segment of the beauty
industry.  Annual expenditure: $8 billion.

Hair?  Seriously?  But just think about it: hair occupies a major position in human existence. Thousands of pages in magazines and newspapers are devoted to hair every month.  Hundreds of songs have included hair in lyrics and titles, not to mention an entire Broadway musical.

In days of old hair length and quality signaled a woman's youth, health, and reproductive potential.  The mystery of hair has been illuminated in the stories of Lady Godiva, Rapunzel, Sampson, and Medusa.  Even the Navajos of the American West give hair supreme significance.  Their legend says that thoughts emerge from one's head along with hair.  The longer the hair one has, the  more thoughts they've had.

Well that's just great.  What about those of us who, whether through genetics, disease, or disease treatment, must live a no-hair life (even if we have hair regrowth in our future)?  Are the myths of youth, health, beauty, intelligence and reproductive potential just not within our reach?  Certainly not.  The secret is to look for the silver lining.  I took my hair loss in my own hands, shaving my head as soon as it started shedding. And I immediately found lots of silver linings as a bald woman.

To start with, my personal hygiene duties were whittled down to almost nothing, and the ensuing time saving was monumental. Here's how I figured it: I washed my hair four times a week (a 5 minute task) and then styled it (at least another 15 minutes). The year I was bald afforded me nearly 70 additional hours to spend on other pursuits. I became very accomplished at Sudoku and crossword puzzles.

In addition I figure my annual hair care expenditure was nearly $1,000 when I tallied up cuts, colors, products, gadgets and paraphernalia. My bald year afforded me a significant savings to be sure. The total, however, was unfortunately reduced by $300 with the purchase of a wig. Big mistake; everyone could tell it was a wig since I kept nervously tugging at it. And it was so hot during the summer months, I felt like I was walking around with a dead cat on my head.

More silver linings: having been a blonde, it was the first time in my life I felt free to laugh at blonde jokes along with my brunette friends. The biggest advantage of all was that weather - the bane of all long-locked gals - is never an issue to a bald woman. I laughed at wind, rain, and humidity, popping a clever hat on my head to keep warm and dry. Once inside again, the hat came off with no trace of hat head.

Humor aside, the point is this: how really significant is hair in the grand scheme of things? Does its style measure your kindness? Does its color make you generous or its texture make you humble? And while I mean no disrespect to Native American culture, can the length of your hair really calculate how deep your thoughts are? Of course not.

We spend far too many hours in our lives trying to impress each other, worrying about things over which we have no control, and worst of all, focusing on things which we will have forgotten a year from now. Anthony J. D'Angelo said, "The most important things in life aren't things."

He's right. It's just a house. It's just a car. And it's just hair.

# Lesson 6:

# Helping Hands

*It's not the load that breaks you down;*
*it's the way you carry it.*
- Lena Horne

"Do by self!" Thus stated my stubborn, three-year-old niece every time she wanted to handle things on her own like a big girl. I totally got the "do-by-self" declaration. After all, I came of age in the 70's when all females of my generation wanted to be independent and liberated. We wanted no interference and no barriers when it came to crawling up the corporate ladder, producing and mothering children, and carving out our place in society. We were quite certain that whatever had been done in previous decades was wrong, and equally certain that admitting the need for assistance signaled weakness. We all knew what happened to animals in the herd perceived as weak: they became the main course for the nearest predator. No, no, not us. We didn't need anyone.

Imagine my surprise then, after being weakened by surgery, chemo and the stress of it all, my Wonder Woman suit no longer fit. Oh, I insisted to all within ear shot that I could still handle everything. I didn't need help with meals, laundry, or gardening. I had always done it. Why should a little cancer slow me down? Those who loved me just shook their heads, wanting so badly to help and wondering when, if ever, I was going to give in. Then I learned something very interesting.

Duke University Medical Center conducted a study, asking former heart patients to visit current heart patients. No particular agenda was suggested, just that they listen and lend support. Afterward, the volunteers were assessed. The results were amazing: the volunteers' health had improved, whereas a control group of other former heart patients who did not volunteer remained the same. It's called "helper's high," a rush of euphoria, followed by a longer period of calm, after performing a kind act. It is an actual, proven, physiological state that has shown up in MRI scans of the brain.

Jordan Grafman, a National Institutes of Health neuroscientist, says, "Those brain structures that are activated when you get a reward are the same ones that are activated when you give. In fact, they're activated more." Additional research shows that "helper's high" can possibly strengthen the immune-system, providing all of the body benefits of stress relief, triggering the body's natural painkillers (endorphins), easing asthma and cardiovascular disease, and helping with weight loss and insomnia.

This is a better health plan than any ever conceived by the U.S. government. Who am I, then, to refuse such benefits to my fellow human beings? Realistically, we really don't do *anything* by ourselves, even in good health. Our very existence is the result of the knowledge and experiences of those who went before us. Why not put on our grown-up panties and ask for help when we need it? Ponder these five additional reasons to do so:

1.  Our world is too complicated to do everything alone. Important or insignificant, everyone needs a helping hand now and then. Get over it.

2.  We all have a front line: someone (or several someones) who care deeply about us. Asking for reinforcements takes the burden not only off us, but off them as well.

3.  Bad news (for those of us who are control freaks): being helped makes us feel indebted. Good news: finding a way to repay that debt down the road could make us grow in ways we hadn't expected.

4.  Sometimes asking for help benefits the helper more than the person on the receiving end. Perhaps they always wanted to feel needed and you were just the person they were waiting for.

5.  Whether you believe in the power of prayer and/ or the power of positive thinking, lots of voices repeating the same thought can't hurt. So ask for good thoughts from those who aren't able to do anything else.

One more thought: sometimes, when we're overwhelmed by our particular burden, we just can't summon the strength to see or talk to people, no matter how loving their gestures may be. That's okay and those who really care about us will understand. There are, however, things that could be done without face to face interactions. They could include creating email blasts to friends and family as updates; sending thank-you notes for gifts, food or flowers; or researching recipes that promote healing for your condition.

This lesson, like many others, is a work in progress for me. Fortunately, these immortal words from Lennon and McCartney keep me on track:

*When I was younger, so much younger than today,*
*I never needed anybody's help in any way*
*But now these days are gone, I'm not so self assured,*
*Now I find I've changed my mind*
*and opened up the doors.*[1]

---

[1] John Lennon and Paul McCartney, "Help!" *Help!* 1965, EMI Studios, London.

# Lesson 7:

# (Don't) Always Be Prepared

*Some people are making such thorough preparations for rainy days that they aren't enjoying today's sunshine.*
- William Feather

*Siempre Listo (Lista)!*

*Toujours Prêt (Prête)!*

*Allzeit bereit!*

These three phrases have one thing in common: they're the Spanish, French and German translations of the Scout motto, "Always be prepared!" Whether or not you were a Scout, my guess is you've surely heard variations of the decree.

As all mothers are, mine was big into preparation for emergencies: "Always have a dime in your shoe so you can call home." "Always wear clean underwear in case you're in a car accident." Remember, we're talking the 1960's and 70's here. Now, no one is ever without a cell phone and most young people wouldn't know how to use a pay phone even if it did still cost a dime. Furthermore questioning underwear condition really isn't relevant today. I fear that an alarmingly large percentage of the population doesn't wear any at all.

Mom's phrases, however, must have worked on me as I am a very prepared person. Dare I say it? I prepare obsessively for everything. My journey from cancer diagnosis through chemo infusions was no different, and I'm not sure access to information via the internet was necessarily a good thing. Travel with me down my road of preparation.

First, I absorbed every shred of information I could find about breast cancer. Big mistake. Most of it scared the hell out of me. Next, I tackled suggestions for surgery and recovery. Take waterless toothbrushes to the hospitals. Check - I bought an economy pack at Costco. Freeze rice in rubbing alcohol and water for use as pliable ice bags when you return home. I made three for good measure, despite the fact that the space they took up in the freezer meant the margarita and piña colada mixes had to be sacrificed.

The chemo warnings included avoiding favorite foods (bad memories would linger in the event of nausea) and stocking up on bland foods. Our refrigerator became so bland, it took on a sad demeanor and after I'd removed the Thai chili sauce and pickled herring, it actually sighed each time it ran. I also made it my mission to be an expert at scarf-tying and wig-wearing (please refer to Lesson 5 about the wig), neither of which are the same with hair as without it.

The *coup de gras*? That would be the day I got all gussied up, complete with false eyelashes, since my own had fallen victim to the chemo treatments. My husband and I were driving 45 miles for dinner with my 96-year-old aunt and mid-trip the corner of one of the lashes popped up. No worries, I thought. I peeled it off with the intention of stopping at the earliest opportunity to buy more glue, but we hit a bump and I dropped the eyelash between the seats. There was nothing else to do but remove the other, perfectly well-positioned lash, and have dinner with bare lids.

The bottom line is that in each instance, I WAY over-prepared. My hospital stay was a scant 28 hours. My recovery? Virtually swelling-free. I threw away the frozen rice bags (still mourning the margarita and piña colada mixes) and gave out the waterless toothbrushes for Halloween. The scarves now have a place around my neck and the wig was donated to charity.

Here's the very important lesson in all of this. When we prepare (or over-prepare), we're visualizing our possible future. My over-preparation not only caused me to visualize worst case scenarios, it also burned up some valuable sunny days. So here's what I'll do in the future; feel free to follow suit.

First and foremost, use your experts, be they doctors, lawyers or hair stylists. You already have an appointment with them, get the most for your money. Take specific, written questions with you and stay on topic. If you don't understand, ask your questions again.

Next while, the internet does provide much information, don't just read the first three results of your Google search, usually the most popular but not necessarily the most accurate in your case. Dig deeper and look for scenarios that are more in line with your own.

Finally, remember that everyone is different. Sometimes when you seek advice, you get more than you want or need. Susan or Debbie's bad result doesn't mean yours will be too. Part of being prepared is preparing for *your* situation. Stay within your parameters.

Napoleon Bonaparte said, "Over-preparation is the foe of inspiration." It's also the foe of reality. Today's assignment: stay focused and stay real.

# Lesson 8:

# Winning *Is* Everything

*Winning isn't everything; it's the only thing.*
- Henry "Red" Sanders

Red Sanders was arguably the best football coach in U.C.L.A history. He won 77% of all the games he coached at the school and, in 1954, led them to their only national championship. He was three times voted collegiate football coach of the year by his peers and inducted into the College Football Hall of Fame. However the thing for which he should be the most famous is sadly attributed to someone else.

Don't get me wrong: Sanders' coaching accomplishments are outstanding. As a die-hard college football fan, I completely get the enormity of his achievements. It's the quote, "Winning isn't everything; it's the only thing," that pulls at my heartstrings. You see, it's Vince Lombardi, not Red Sanders, who is commonly given credit for it. That quote has great significance in the lives of those facing life challenges, and I think we should get it right. Let me explain.

I'm not certain when I first associated myself with the words "cancer survivor." It's kind of like turning 50. You know it's out there, you're marching toward it, and then one day, you're there. Of course, arriving at cancer survivorship is always a good thing. Turning 50? It has its pros and cons.

Evidently, the concept of "cancer survivor" is big business. A Google search returns over 33 million websites pertaining to the phrase, a list that includes survivor networks, organizations, and projects. The first Sunday in June has been proclaimed National Cancer Survivor Day, and their website promises a merchandise catalogue is coming soon. There are cancer survivor tattoos and even cancer survivor scholarships. It is, by all accounts, the commonly accepted (and certainly hoped for) status someone with cancer aspires to. But it's all wrong.

The Merriam-Webster online dictionary defines survivor as "remaining alive or in existence" and "continuing to function." That sounds more like a description of our 15-year-old washing machine than the result of body-altering surgery and 18 rounds of chemotherapy.

Those of us with cancer are said to "fight" our disease. We "battle" it with all that modern medicine can throw at it. The dictionary defines a fight this way: "To strive vigorously and resolutely; to contend with physically or in battle." An army fights an enemy. Red Sanders's football teams fought to win games. And in both scenarios, when those fighters were triumphant, they were called winners (defined as "achieving success in an effort or venture" and "finishing first in a competition").

Imagine the response you'd receive if you congratulated a general for his troops' "survival" over their foes. And if you'd dumped the water cooler on Red for "surviving" his game against U.C.L.A.'s arch rival

U.S.C., I suspect you would have been thanked with a black eye. Neither of those leaders would tolerate being told they were "survivors." They were winners!

I didn't set out to survive cancer; I set out to beat it. Consequently, I don't want to be a "cancer survivor." I am a "cancer winner." Doesn't that sound far more powerful and positive? As any coach or general or doctor will tell you, it's the power in a positive attitude that enables people to win. And winning life's challenges *is* everything.

# Lesson 9:

# Making a List, Checking It Twice

*We have no right to ask when sorrow comes, "Why did this happen to me?" unless we ask the same question for every moment of happiness that comes our way.*
- Author Unknown

Human beings love the number 10. It symbolizes the completion of a cycle, the culmination of the numbers that come before it and the start of a whole new order of numbers coming after it. Whether or not it's because we have 10 fingers and 10 toes (making counting convenient), 10 is the basis of monetary, decimal, and metric systems. In advertisements the time displayed on a watch is frequently 10:10. It frames the watchmaker's logo, precisely where the advertiser wants us to look.

And who among us isn't familiar with Top 10 Lists? While the first might have been the one Moses received (otherwise known as the Ten Commandments), it was David Letterman's Top 10 List, which debuted in September of 1985, that really got the ball rolling. The lists are everywhere, a vehicle for the best, worst, most, and least.

Soon after I was diagnosed with breast cancer, a very dear friend, who'd seen her share of dark days, told me about about a Top 10 List she had. At a time when she had felt the very lowest, she forced herself to sit down and write out the 10 things she was most grateful for. As distraught as she was, it was a struggle, a task she had to leave and return to several times in order to complete. Once she had finished, she made multiple copies and put one in her purse, one at her desk, and one in her nightstand. She told me she reads her list each time she feels as though life is unfair and nothing is going right, and she adds to it as other blessings come to mind, sometimes making it her Top 20 List.

What a great idea! Now for a reality check. When we learn about exercises like this, when we read statements that tell us to look for the bright side of a situation and to count our blessings, our minds give us every reason to embrace the theories. Our hearts, however, are another matter. To use myself as an example,in my heart (and in my reflection in the mirror), I saw a pitiful, hairless, one-boobed woman, who was spending her summer days cradling the toilet. Poor, shallow little me.

I made the stupid list anyway and its effect surpised me to the core. I'm sharing it with you here for two reasons. One, maybe some of my items fit your life. Feel free to plagiarize them for your list if you need to. More importantly, when you put something forward in public, you have no choice but to live up to it. If you ever hear me complaining about my life, give me a punch and tell me to go back to my list.

## The Top 10 Blessings in My Life

*10. The roof over my head and food in my kitchen.*

*9. My physical fitness before the cancer (which I will return to!)*

*8. My strength in the face of this horrible disease.*

*7. My sense of humor.*

*6. The lessons my parents taught me.*

*5. The freedoms I enjoy as an American.*

*4. The skills of writing and public speaking.*

*3. The beauty in the world around me.*

*2. The love and health of my children, grand-children, family and friends.*

*And my #1 blessing: The love and honor of my husband.*


My friend's idea was one of the most useful things I did during my journey. Here's what happened (and continues to happen today). Every time I go back to poor, shallow little me, I find my list, read it and realize the items on it are things no disease can ever take from me. I keep several copies of it handy. I don't care that my list will never make a hit TV show like *Late Night with David Letterman*. It's the "hit" to my spirit that's important whenever I need a reminder of what a wonderful world I live in.

# Lesson 10:

# Global Warning

*Reality is merely an illusion, albeit a very persistent one.*
- Albert Einstein

When I was a child, I loved snow globes. They were
magical worlds whose atmospheric conditions you could
affect with a mere shake. I had one that snowed on
Mother Goose characters and another that, made to look
like the sea, dropped silver shavings on three suspended
fish. A third one had a Halloween theme, and the fourth
was of a city, brought back from a trip my parents had
taken.

Sadly my childhood carelessness, and that of my
children, along with a number of cross-country moves,

has depleted my collection of snow globes. I'm down to just the fish in the sea, and they're looking a little shabby.

It was the image of a snow globe that popped into my mind a few days after my cancer diagnosis. There was a new snow globe in my life and I was in it. I could see out and my friends and family could see in, but we were suddenly separated by a distinct barrier. I had entered a world apart from them. Not that I wanted them to join me in my new globe-world, but the isolation I felt was very real. And as time went on, it got worse.

My fears (I might die; chemotherapy will melt the skin off my body), along with my feelings (I'll be a disfigured freak; I'll never be pretty) floated around in the globe like the fishes' silver shavings, reproducing on an alarming basis. My repeated attempts to convey these fears and feelings to my loved ones were met with blank stares, as if I was speaking a different language. They kept patting my hand (literally and figuratively), telling me how beautiful and courageous I was. Their insistence that I possessed such qualities only made my anxieties grow, as if an evil spell was causing them to believe such nonsense about me.

A case in point: there was a sizable gap in understanding between my youngest son and me over the issue of chemotherapy. His position was that since the doctors reported all cancer had been removed at the time of surgery, he didn't want me to put my body - and my mind - through such poisonous ravages. I responded that, after learning that my recurrence rate was 30% without chemotherapy, not having it was out of the question. It was gonna happen, regardless of the side effects. The more we discussed it, the more we each dug in our heels.

I now realize my family and friends had a slate of fears and feelings totally different from mine. None of them ever thought I was going to die; apparently only I had gotten that message. Rather, they didn't want me to have to endure the physical pain and mental stress from tests and treatments. Beyond that, their feelings about me as the person they knew and loved hadn't changed. Nonetheless, as determined as they were to make me understand their perspectives, I was just as determined to make them understand mine. It was akin to a Congressional debate, where both sides of the aisle contend their position on an issue is the only possible truth.

Lest you think I have a dangerously over-active imagination, or you're leaning toward pity for me because of an obvious mental disorder, I have learned that my "in the globe/out of the globe" illusion is neither crazy nor my own. I've met others who had the same fantasy.

When you choose to embrace hair loss as I did, you are a walking billboard with the message, "I am undergoing (or have undergone) chemotherapy." Since more women have breast cancer than any other type, those who saw me assumed that's the club I belonged to. I was astounded and touched by the number of complete strangers who approached me. They told me they remembered all too well their entry into the sisterhood. Invariably, the conversation would get around to our families' involvement in our disease. Without exception, all of them agreed it was nearly impossible to make loved ones accept what had become our reality, and vice-versa.

Ah, acceptance: the condition we all wish we possessed, when, in the real world, it's a struggle every day on every level. Now that this experience is in my rear view mirror, I see clearly that my loved ones and I would *never* have been able to convert one another. And so it is with many life challenges. No matter how badly we want to express support and empathy for someone we care about, unless we've lived through the same crisis, we can't ever truly walk in their shoes. Even if we have had a similar situation, no one ever experiences life in exactly the same way. We still wouldn't have walked in their shoes.

There is a healthier and more productive course to follow, one which I'm going to apply the next time I find myself in a snow globe situation, no matter which side of the glass I'm on. First, allow those in the globe to air their laundry, no matter how difficult it is to hear. Don't agree or disagree, don't make suggestions, just let 'em get it out there. Then ask them if you can give them your observations, not because yours are right or better, but because you care about them, and therefore have a dog in the hunt, too. Ask them to follow the same "get it out there" rules that you observed for them, no matter how hard it is for them to just sit and listen. Finally, agree that honoring one another's truths is the most important goal. By not creating a conflict between you, there's more energy for all of you to fight the real battle.

By the way, I'm happy to report that my snow globe collection has once again been reduced. One day, I don't even know which one, the snow globe which had appeared with my diagnosis, disappeared. So while the three fish still swim among the silver shavings in the globe from my childhood, my family, friends and I are all back together in one world.

# Lesson 11:

# Get Ready ... Get Set ...

*All glory comes from daring to begin.*
- Eugene F. Ware

... and suddenly the screech of brakes. You had every intention of moving ahead. You had a long talk with yourself and were quite certain of your plan. Everything seemed in place, but then, your feet - or whatever body part was required - were a no-show. You just couldn't do it. You are not alone.

Nary a person on the planet over the age of 5 is without such an experience. My father must have had plenty of them, as he was always ready with this advice when he saw I was afraid to move forward: suck it up and get on with it. The sooner you start, the sooner it will be over. Not exactly a foolproof set of instructions to remove the death grip fear had on my heart.

It's fear that stops us dead in our tracks at the thought of taking on a life-threatening disease. It's fear that makes us want to hide under the covers (preferably with a box of donuts or a bottle of Jack Daniels) rather than face an adversary. It's fear that is the little voice in our head, telling us that what we're about to do could turn out very badly, and is therefore something we should avoid. Fear is an emotion, and all emotions are an impulse to act. Fear's message to the brain is to do one of two things, either imitate a deer in headlights (even *inaction* is an action) or run like hell in the other direction.

Three main fears most often haunt our lives, sinister demons under whose protection all others exist: the fear of failure, the fear of change, and the fear of the unknown. While they may rise up individually, they frequently become one ugly package when we're confronted by a major, life altering challenge. I was not exempt.

As soon as I was diagnosed with cancer, my fears arrived in full form. They roared into my life, with their bags packed, like a visit from unwanted relatives (picture the Clampetts, complete with Granny in the rocking chair). And it appeared they were moving in for the long haul. All the many, lonely hours I spent undergoing diagnostic tests in MRI, CAT, and PET scan tubes, my family of fears was crowded in there with me.

Being a student of history, and to squelch my fears' unrelenting chatter on one test day, I thought of people who had faced down big events - people whose actions had had world-changing outcomes. How did the guys about to land on the Normandy beaches feel, just before their boats hit shore on D-Day in 1944? What about the black students, who, in 1963, prepared to register at the all-white University of Alabama? Where were the astronauts' thoughts as their lunar module was about to touch down on the moon in 1969? Suddenly, my little MRI that day seemed much less significant.

How about a better way to face down fear? Look at it for what it really is, and then come up with a game plan for handling it. As I began to do that, the following action list evolved, cobbled together from internet research, advice from others and my own thoughts.

1. **This one is really important: our fear is usually born from how we think we'll feel when something happens to us.** It's not reality based; it's the fear of the unknown. Re-read Lesson 2 if you need a refresher on that.

2. **It's okay to be afraid.** It's normal. Everyone gets a pass now and then, and the bigger the challenge, the more passes you get. Give yourself permission to be afraid.

3. **Assemble a collection of resources.** Find books, websites, and real people, those with real knowledge and training within the realm of your challenge. If it's illness you're facing, find someone who's had the same illness, at the same stage, who underwent the same treatment. Get them to tell you what taking the first step was like. Doctors and other health professionals always have lists of resources. Ask for them.

4. **Take your time in making decisions.** We live in a fast-paced world with lots of options. Sometimes we're tempted to leap before we look.

In most cases, even for those involving a dire diagnosis like cancer, a delay of a a few days won't change the outcome of the treatment. Ask questions, get a second opinion, and if the professional you're working with doesn't float your boat, find one who does. It's your life.

5. **Don't go it alone.** Loneliness only adds one more layer of fear to an already stressful situation. Take someone to appointments with you who can act as another set of eyes and ears. Have a short list of people you can call day or night just to touch base. Remember Lesson 6? There is no shame in asking for help.

I have no doubt that my dear daddy's recommended plan of action worked for him. The list I made worked for me. Neither may be your cup of tea. The important thing is not to believe that fear is unbeatable. Think about what will best enable you to take the first step. Then get ready ... get set ... go!

# Lesson 12:

# An Apple a Day

*Act as if what you do makes a difference. It does.*
- William James

As a person of extreme action I've never been able to let a minute lapse without being productive in some way. In fact, the only reason I sleep at night is because my wrinkle cream jar says, "Works while you sleep." I figure if I don't sleep, it won't work, and I just don't want to take that chance.

So there I was one day, gliding into an MRI tube for more diagnostic tests. I really hate those scans, not because I'm claustrophobic, but because they mean 45 plus minutes of lying absolutely still, listening to clunks and grinds. The only production I'm capable of, then, is thinking and here's where my thoughts led me on that particular day.

Everyone is familiar with the story of Sir Issac Newton. The version most of us know is that an apple fell on his head and gravity suddenly became a buzz word. Makes for a cute image, but here's the accurate account, as recorded by Newton's friend and first biographer. Having tea in the garden one day, Newton mused out loud to his friend that the reason the apples fell off his trees in a downward direction, rather than upward or sideways, must be the result of some drawing power, pulling them toward the earth's center. That single thought nudged Newton to produce a universe-altering principle, still held as a truth 300 centuries later.

What if all the things that happen to us in a lifetime are also nudges toward something bigger? A woman stops to tie her shoe one day before entering a crosswalk, thereby avoiding an out-of-control truck failing to heed the stop sign. That leaves her unharmed to continue to the library, where she sees a child learning to read. She suggests a favorite childhood book of her own to the child's mother. The lesson in the book sparks an interest in the child, and the flame grows along with the child's shoe size. Upon becoming an adult, he or she discovers a vaccine that eradicates cancer. An entire segment of the world's population lives to go on to do other great things, and save other segments of the population. And it all began when the woman stopped to tie her shoe.

Nudges that result in greatness happen to all of us, often when we least expect them. Josephine Billings, a lifelong volunteer advocate for improving health care, said, "To the world you may be just one person. But to one person, you may be the world." What if the consequences of our life challenges are as important as the day that woman stopped to tie her shoe? What if they're an exercise to make us better, or the world better?

As I said earlier, we all face life challenges. They're the things that make us barely able to function some days. Rising from bed in the morning is a near impossibility. Sometimes, we can't fathom any reason to continue. But somewhere there are people who need you. They may be your closest companion or you may not even know them.

Because of you and your present situation, however, their life will be enhanced. They, in turn, could enhance others' lives, and so on. What an awesome responsibility.

Lying in the MRI tube that day, I scanned through my memory bank looking for other events in my life that were nearly as difficult and down right scary as the cancer I was battling. Then I fast-forwarded and found positive events that had been nudged into reality as a result of my difficulties. They weren't commensurate with the discovery of gravity, but they were important in the lives of those dear to me, and maybe others I didn't even know about. Clearly they wouldn't have happened if I hadn't been challenged in the first place.

What events have occurred in your life that were major pains at the outset? Where did they lead you, and who did they lead you to? How are you and others better off for the experiences? Remember this: never think that something as horrible as cancer, or as insignificant as an apple falling from a tree, can't have an enormously positive affect on the world and the future.

# Lesson 13:

# Keep Calm and Carry On

*If you want to test your memory, try to recall what*
*you were worrying about one year ago today.*
- E. Joseph Cossman

I have long been interested in World War II era
history, but never imagined that such interest would find
its way into this chapter of my life. While strolling past
London souvenir shops, during our trip to Britain prior to
my surgery, an image repeatedly jumped out at me.
Coffee mugs and tee shirts, key chains and coasters, all
boasted the same catchy phrase: "Keep calm and carry
on." How perfectly ironic.

A researcher to the core, I checked into the origin of
the phrase. In 1939, just prior to the onset of the war in
Europe, the British Ministry of Information published a

series of three posters. They were to become, as one of the creators put it, "a rallying war-cry that will bring out the best in every one of us and put us in an offensive mood at once."

The "keep calm" poster was the third in the series, and not nearly as popular as the others at the time. It was re-discovered at the beginning of this century, and now garners attention in ways its originators never dreamed of. Its appearance in my life at this particular time could mean only one thing: the message was meant especially for me.

**Keep Calm.** Ha, sure, while everything crumbles around me. I have cancer and my kid's going to war, for God's sake. What other little nuggets of inspiration might find their way into my sphere? Keeping calm was not gonna happen to me for a long time. But then I took a closer look at some of the information I'd been reading about how to defeat cancer, my new enemy. Keeping calm, a.k.a. stress-busting, was high on the list.

More research. Experts agree some stress is a good thing; it keeps us on our toes. Stress management, not stress elimination, is what we should strive for. Sadly, however, it appears most of us aren't very good managers. The ensuing medical problems caused by being over-stressed can be greater than the issue that stressed us out in the first place.

When we're threatened, our bodies go on autopilot, summoning up what was needed eons ago to kcep us alive in the wilderness. Powerful hormones are released, intended only for short-term duty in emergency situations. When the threat passes, different chemicals are released to bring us back into balance.

Problem is, if we are constantly stressed, the calming hormones are never released and our bodies suffer. Cells in the brain responsible for memory and learning are injured or destroyed. Cardiovascular disease and high blood pressure crop up. The immune system is suppressed, making us more susceptible to infection and illness, and an alarming cycle begins. We get sick, we become stressed about it, we get sicker, we become more stressed, and so on. It's really bad for your health. No kidding.

What to do, what to do? A Mayo Clinic web page offered ten ideas: get active, meditate, laugh, connect with others, assert yourself, do yoga, sleep, journal, get musical, seek counsel.[2] But probably their best advice is, like a buffet, you don't have to stick with just one thing. If something doesn't work, try another, or do a combination. I went the buffet route, with success, I might add. The bottom line is that, as patients, we have responsibility in getting ourselves healthy again. Keeping calm is a big one.

**Carry On.** I figured this part of the poster out for myself, since carrying on is what this book is all about. Facing and fighting against a challenge, like cancer, is a marathon, not a sprint. So is life. We are capable of thinking, talking, dreaming, and breathing in the face of enormous adversity. Trying to keep things real, trying to carry on, plays back into the idea of keeping calm. It's about recognizing what we have to live for, and planning the legacy we'll leave behind. We hope, of course, that the "leaving behind" part comes later rather than sooner

---

[2] Mayo Clinic, http://www.mayoclinic.com/health/stress-relievers/MY01373

for us, but planning ahead is good medicine, too. It gives us even more reason to carry on.

When that fellow said these posters would be "a rallying war-cry that will bring out the best in every one of us and put us in an offensive mood at once," I'm quite sure he never thought about them having the same effect on those of us facing life challenges. Isn't irony ironic?

# Lesson 14:

# Buddy, Can You
# Spare Some Change?

*Change is inevitable - except from a vending machine.*
- Robert Gallagher

From books to movies, you can find dozens of characters who long for the good old days. They reminisce about how things used to be, before they changed. Like me, you probably have friends and relatives who wax on about the negative aspects of change, too. I used to think only the old fogies were against change. Now I realize that either the "change complainers" are getting younger, or my contemporaries have become old fogies.

If there is one universal truth, though, it is this: change happens. Period. Once again, we might as well put on our grown-up panties and deal with it. It occurs in our personal lives as well as our professional lives, and it certainly makes an appearance when we face life challenges. You just can't go through something really big, and not be changed by it, unless you were unconscious the entire time. Even then, the world you face upon regaining consciousness would have changed without you, and you'd be forced to catch up.

Our society has instilled in us a very peculiar notion that appears to be the root of our contempt for change. It's the idea that we want to know, in advance, the answers and outcomes to everything before we even start. We want to count on those thing as absolutes, a form of security blanket. If things are changed, the answers and outcomes will be changed, too, and we'll be adrift in an unknown sea. (Remember Lesson 2?)

A catastrophic life event, like the loss of a job or a potentially fatal disease, changes us from the start. What we had relied on as permanent, the existence of that job or our health, has suddenly been proven to be unstable. Secondly, grief emotions - anger, guilt, denial, and depression - make an appearance. Upon hearing my diagnosis, I was very angry, since I'd spent most of my adult life exercising and eating healthily. Then I felt guilty about the times I had fallen off the health wagon with french fries or too much wine. Had my weaknesses caused the disease? Finally, I sank into the deep end of the "I'll never be the same" depression pool. Then I discovered this.

It is said that the Chinese word for change is made up of two characters: one meaning danger, the other meaning opportunity. This may or may not be true, but it doesn't matter. What does matter is that there are definitely two ways to look at change  Traveling this cancer road, I've met lots of women who have battled against breast cancer. Some of them, even though they have been given a clean bill of health, fear that they may fall victim to the disease again. Every breath they take is a trembling sigh. The sad reality is that their inability to embrace the changes that happened to them has already made them victims of the disease for a second time.

On the other hand, the changes we experience from cancer, divorce, bankruptcy, and so on, bring us face to face with people, organizations, books, and lifestyles we would NEVER have encountered in our old lives. Those could indeed be opportunities, if we're willing to see them as a sign that we're about to move in a different direction, rather than simply as a stop sign.

There's a tool I've used often in my life to get ready for something important: visualization. It's not a weirded-out science, but rather a powerful way to prepare yourself for future events. Top athletes use it before games; successful business people use it before tough negotiations; politicians use it before delivering speeches. It's simple, cheap and it works. And it's a great tool for coping with change.

Before my surgery, I imagined what I would be like a few weeks after it was all over. The incision would be healed, my strength would be coming back, and a big hunk of cancer would be out of my life forever. My doctors would tell me how well I was recovering. My husband and children would be proud of me. Even the looming specter of chemotherapy got in the act. Yes, the visualized me was tired and got sick, but I always looked fabulous as a bald woman. (This was no doubt aided by my limited knowledge of graphics manipulation: I cut and pasted my face on internet images of bald female celebrities. I looked pretty good.) I'm not going to say I wasn't scared to death through the whole ordeal, but the visualization, having made me familiar with the scene, certainly took an edge off my fear of the changes awaiting me.

Let's be real: there's no way any of us can ever escape change, even when we're not facing the big stuff. We can either wallow in fear and agonize over it, or prepare for it and try to find something positive in it. Still not convinced? Think of it this way. If nothing ever changed, right now you could be sitting in front of your goatskin tent, cooking stew made of questionable ingredients, in an unclean pot over a fire fueled by dried animal dung. Now, do you really want to bash change?

# Lesson 15:

# Welcome to My Nightmare

*The sincere friends of this world are as ship lights
in the stormiest of nights.*
- Giotto di Bondone

A while ago - I assume in an attempt to liven up what might otherwise be another dull day in the classroom - college professors across the country presented "The Last Lecture." The concept was simple: they were to consider their demise and what mattered most to them in the world and then tell their story. As the professors spoke, it was hoped that their audiences would mull over the same "what if's." What an interesting new spin in modern education. But I'm quite certain that those who conceived it never saw Randy Pausch coming.

Pausch was a brilliant computer science professor at Carnegie Mellon University. He was widely respected in academic and business circles alike. He, too, was asked to deliver a "last lecture." But he didn't have to use much imagination to put it together. A month earlier, doctors had told him he had three to six months to live. Then he would die of pancreatic cancer.

Pausch's lecture, delivered in September 2007 and entitled "Really Achieving Your Childhood Dreams," travels the gamut of emotions. He was self-deprecating, thought-provoking and funny. Midway through he had a birthday cake brought out for his wife and encouraged the entire lecture hall to sing to her. The tears flowed, mine at my computer as I watched, as well as those of everyone filling the Carnegie Mellon venue. But the most amazing line in the one hour and 15 minute lecture was the last one. "This talk's not for you," Pausch tells the audience, "it's for my kids."

Wow. Here's a guy with an amazing skill set, given the chance to toot his own horn and impress the world with his knowledge one final time. Instead, he uses the opportunity to deliver a lesson to his children, then ages six, three and two, knowing they had been pulled into his nightmare through no fault of their own. And he knew it was going to get much worse for them. Furthermore, I think he realized he had a lot of parenting to do, and not a lot of time in which to do it.

You see, when fate delivers us an unexpected life challenge that becomes a nightmare, we are not the only affected party. A wave of pain and sorrow reaches our entire sphere of influence, the greatest of which is felt by those who love us the most. They look for ways to make us more comfortable, to help us through the dark passage. It quickly becomes all about us: *we* are the patient; *we* are the victim; *we* are the focus of all their attention and energy.

But hold the phone. While *we* are becoming the center of the universe, those caring for us are taking on extra burdens, both physically and emotionally. They're giving up a great deal, too. According to the National Center on Care Giving, care givers might neglect their own health, take on feelings of loneliness or isolation, miss work, and become depressed.

So here's where I'm going with this. In Lesson 6, I told you it was important to let people help you, because it makes them feel good. The reverse is also true. It's good for you to help those helping you. Can't muster enough energy to take on big chores? That's okay. Small efforts count.

While I was experiencing all the thrills of cancer and chemotherapy, I never stopped writing. I wrote newsletters and blogs and magazine columns. When I didn't feel like making complete sentences, I wrote phases and words in a journal. I sent out lots of emails. Some of them dealt with my illness. All of them included humor. My family and friends told me afterward that my words kept their spirits up. Ta-da! I was helping the helpers.

The public evidence of Randy Pausch helping his helpers was his lecture. I have no doubt that he never expected it to become as large as it has; he just doesn't appear like the kind of guy who'd use cancer as a publicity stunt. Rather, I think he saw it as an advance opportunity to say thank you to those who had joined him in his nightmare, those who cared for him, those who loved him. His lesson is the same as the one here: take care of those with you in your nightmare.

# Lesson 16:

# Ten Reps of Patience

*Have patience with all things; but first of all with yourself.*
- St. Francis de Sales

Let's just get it out there: I am not a patient woman. Patience is not a virtue in my war chest. Charity and justice? Absolutely! Courage? Giving it my best shot. But patience tries my patience. As a child, I remember rebukes from both my parents and my teachers regarding my lack of the "p" word. I seriously doubt that, at this stage in my life, a big helping of patience is going to fill an otherwise unused portion of my brain.

Patience, itself, has a healthy resumé. It's mentioned on many a virtue list - including those of the Greeks and Romans as well as in Eastern and Western religions. I'm sorry to say I'm probably more familiar with the opposites of patience, those being from the same virtue lists: wrath, conflict, hostility, and suffering. In fact, the anti-patience characteristics are the very emotions that tend to bubble to the surface first for me, while I frantically search for the pocket in which I've stuffed my patience.

We live in a world where everything is instant. Lights, television sets and dishwashers turn on with the press of a button. Communications - in the form of texts, emails, and cell phone calls - happen from one corner of the world to another in a matter of seconds. We can even find dating prospects on the internet in less time than it takes to change the oil in our cars.

Conversely, patience is required in abnormal quantities when dealing with a life challenge. We recognize the need for professional practitioners (doctors, lawyers, etc.) in the time of crisis, but must *wait* until they can fit us into their calendars. We *wait* in their aptly named *waiting* rooms, while they finish speaking with other people, who had also *waited* for them. When we do get our chance to discuss our issues with them, or to be examined, as the case may be, we must further *wait* for their thoughts and recommendations before proceeding to our next step. Without a doubt, the next step will require more *waiting* and patience.

After a great deal of what felt like running in place following my cancer diagnosis, my surgeon's office called with a date for my surgery. It was 53 days after the diagnosis had initially been made. The increase in my blood pressure must have been audible through the phone. Be patient, they said. We need more tests, they said. Your health is not in danger, nor would we ever let it be, they said. Meanwhile, I felt as though I'd had cancer most of my life, and that it was eating its way through my body like a posse of PacMen.

It occurs to me now that testing one's patience is a test of one's courage, as well. It's far easier to give up than hang in there. The hanging on is the courageous part, and it's been going on for a long time. Did you know that designs for the printing press date back to 200 AD, but a modern version didn't appear until 1439? Or that the first published design for a submarine was in 1573, but they weren't used in naval combat until 1776? Or that light bulb experimentation started in 1802, but the invention of a modern light bulb didn't happen until 1879?

If all these inventions could hang on for centuries before being realized, surely we can muster patience to hang on over a period of days, weeks, months, even years, to overcome our challenges and reach our goals. I devised this little list in my journal one day to remind myself to be more patient.

1. Look at the big picture and see it from as many angles as you can.
2. Patient people live better lives. Being impatient causes stress and that's a bad thing.
3. Remember, you only have what you've been given to work with, no matter how much you wish you had more.
4. Remember what really matters.
5. You will always get what you need, which is sometimes more important than what you want. (When in doubt on this one, refer back to #4.)

As with many other things in life, I'm guessing my patience will become stronger the more I practice it, kind of like doing reps at the gym. I admit it's not easy. But I see a little more clearly how important it will be to have my patience in better form the next time a challenge enters my life.

# Lesson 17:

# Blessings Count

*Be kinder than necessary. Everyone you meet
is fighting some kind of battle.*
- John Watson

The last day of our Pre-Surgery/Pre-Deployment family trip to England was spent in London. We did a number of tourist things as a group, and then everyone split up to put last minute checks on their British vacation to-do list. There was nothing left on my to-do list. Rather, I was anxiously watching the minutes fly by, mentally counting them down till my surgery. Forty-eight hours to go. Then my chest would be ripped open, and the size of the beast growing inside would be known to all. Dramatic? Yes, but I was starting to feel the terror, and that tends to bring out the drama in anyone.

So I wandered around, taking in the vivid sights and sounds of that great city on a perfect spring day. I suddenly found myself standing in front of the small, unassuming Parish Church of St. Michael's Cornhill. The strains of a choir reached out through its open doors and beckoned me in. The church is not large by European cathedral standards, and its architecture is decidedly unique. Replacing the customary cold, gray stone, St. Michael's columns and floor are pure white. And the ceiling is the color of a robin's egg: a happy, blue-green shade that just makes you smile.

I sat down in one of the carved back pews, still soaking up my surroundings, listening to the ethereal voices of the choir when I saw it. Floating there, over the alter, as majestic as the subject it displayed: a stained glass window, bearing a representation of "Christ in Glory." Since the spring sun was high in the clear sky outside, the colors were so luminous they were almost painful to look it. This is it, I thought. This is the image I'm going to bring to mind as I'm drifting off on the operating table.

While we often make promises to ourselves and promptly forget them, this was one I kept. I chatted nervously about that beautiful stained glass window until the anesthesiologist clamped the breathing mask over my face.

Fast forward six months. My surgery had healed, my chemo was behind me, and we were going to England again. We couldn't fill the shoes of my son, still in Afghanistan, but we could at least brighten up Christmas for our daughter-in-law and grandchildren. Midway through our visit, my husband and I returned to London, and I made a beeline for St. Michael's. I wanted to see again what had been such an inspiration on the scariest day of my life.

The church narthex was busy; a woman filled punch cups on a table spread with Christmas cookies, while others set out programs and literature. They asked if I was attending the evening's choir event. I told them I wasn't and only wanted to spend a few minutes in the sanctuary, which they welcomed me to do. While it was as lovely as I remembered, the stained glass window, to my disappointment, was barely visible. I hadn't considered the time of day, nor the time of year. Darkness comes early during British winters, and the window was its victim: a dark gray disk on the wall above the alter.

The time certainly could have better spent, but I still felt moved to make a small donation. I returned to the narthex to ask the punch lady (a woman about my age) how I might do that. She looked at me quizzically and I explained my connection to the church, finishing with, "It's been kind of a tough year."

She patted my shoulder knowingly. I expected to hear a cluck of sympathy from her, but instead she told me her story. On nearly the very same day as my surgery, her husband of 35 years kissed her goodbye and went off to work in the morning. But rather than drive to his office, he drove to a nearby park and shot himself dead.

The woman told me he didn't leave a note of explanation nor could she begin to fathom why he had done it. They had always been happy, not in any financial distress, and had been blessed with a grown son, a beautiful daughter-in-law and a cherished granddaughter. With the Christmas season in full swing, while all the rest of us were relishing our family traditions, she was handling their traditions by herself: putting up the lights, listening to the carols, working on the holiday events at St. Michael's.

There are moments in our lives that seem overwhelming, moments that we're certain are darker than anyone else has ever seen. Yet, we can be assured, there are others whose moments are darker still. Each of us could tell a story such as this. And we should do so at every opportunity, not only to remind ourselves to count our blessings, but as a reminder to whoever is listening to do the same.

This lovely woman made me realize that my trip to St. Michael's was not time wasted. Rather, it was a lesson in how really blessed my life is.

# Lesson 18:

# A Guy Goes to See His Doctor ...

*If I had no sense of humor,*
*I would long ago have committed suicide.*
- Mahatma Ghandi

... and the doctor says, "The tests show that your cancer is advanced. You only have six months to live." The guy is distraught and replies, "But doctor, I won't be able to pay off my medical bills in six months." The doctor thinks for a minute and tells him, "In that case, you have 12 months to live."

I can hear it now: gasps of horror. Everyone knows cancer is no laughing matter. Neither is divorce or unemployment or the death of a loved one. I know, I've experienced them all. However, that doesn't mean that laughter isn't good medicine for them. Fortunately, my family passes along a humor gene. I can't remember an instance of extreme stress that we haven't relieved with a little levity. Lest you think we are a clan of unsympathetic oafs, let me lay a little research on you.

Studies being done in multiple countries, including the United States, have taken on the science of human laughter: what it is, why we do it and what's in it for us. Evidence is mounting that proves it's not just a distraction, it's physically good for us as well. The act of laughing, and producing our familiar "ha, ha, ha" sounds, creates muscle exertion, which in turn triggers a release of endorphins, the feel-good hormones. Those same hormones also relieve pain. They're the ones that show up at our workouts, allow us to do more and feel really good about ourselves afterwards. Like working out, laughter stretches our facial and abdominal muscles, causing us to breath more heavily. This, in turn, pumps more oxygen into our bodies, benefiting hearts, lungs and the rest of our organs. We burn calories when we laugh, too.

Even the Mayo Clinic is on board. According to the clinic's website:

> *"Negative thoughts manifest into chemical reactions that can impact your body by bringing more stress into your system and decreasing your immunity. In contrast, positive thoughts actually release neuropeptides that help fight stress and potentially more serious illnesses."*[3]

Okay, so laughter is good for us. Does that mean we laugh at all those facing challenges and those who are less fortunate? Of course not. It's not in the *person* that we look for humor; it's in the *situation*. Situations jumped out and grabbed me at every turn in my cancer treatment and recovery, and I gladly shared them with all who would listen. After all, if we can have a sense of humor about our situation, those who love and care for us can lighten up, too. Wouldn't you rather be with someone who can still manage a smile, even in the midst of darkness? The great comedian, Bill Cosby, makes a good point: "You can turn painful situations around

---

[3] Mayo Clinic, http://www.mayoclinic.com/health/stress-relief/SR00034

through laughter. If you can find humor in anything, even poverty, you can survive it."

There were dozens of times that my family and I laughed at my situation. To illustrate them here would serve no purpose. They all fall into the "you had to be there" category. But we'll remember them, and I figure we'll pull them out and dust them off the next time we find ourselves in a sticky situation.

By the way, how lucky are you in this day and age! If humor isn't in your nature, or your gene structure, you can go find someone who does it for a living. Rent movies, read short stories, actively look for something humorous with which to distract yourself. Take a vacation from all that's on your plate, even if it's only in your mind.

The point is this: in the hospital they give you ice chips to quench your thirst after surgery. Think of humor the same way. Together with those who love you, find some little chips and use them to quench your thirst for happier days.

# Lesson 19:

# Courage Is Contagious

*We gain strength and courage and confidence by each experience in which we really stop to look fear in the face... we must do that which we think we cannot.*
- Eleanor Roosevelt

Of all the curious and unexpected experiences I had during my cancer saga, the most astonishing kept happening over and over again. Family, friends and complete strangers alike told me I was courageous, a statement I resolutely denied.

I have spent more than a decade researching, interviewing and writing about courageous people: those I considered REALLY courageous. They had fought in wars, gone undercover as spies, risen up against oppression. They had done grand things, been outstanding examples of courage in the service of their fellow human beings. I just had a little breast cancer. My focus wasn't on saving the world, it was on trying to save *me*. Those who thought I was courageous were clearly delusional, but their accusations continued. So I dug out research on the subject for the book I had been working on, and began to reread what I had forgotten in the flurry of my diagnosis.

Courage has been studied and written about with great fervor for centuries. Greek philosopher Aristotle listed it as one of the principal virtues of the human race. He was intrigued by it, and appears to have started the ensuing search for its meaning. While many have taken a stab at understanding it, a single problem remains. Courage is difficult to define and impossible to measure. Unlike taking one's temperature or blood pressure, we have no apparatus to assess its size, shape or volume. We can, however, calculate that which is considered the antithesis of courage: fear.

In their search for the meaning of courage, then, experts have measured fear, collectively coming up with the notion that fearless people are not courageous people. Without the gut-wrenching, knuckle-whitening, sweat-producing, heart-palpitating sensations that fear produces, completing a courageous act would be no different than completing any other act. If snakes don't bother you, then playing with them isn't courageous. Stretching beyond your fear is what makes you courageous. In other words, courage isn't the absence of fear; it's the management of fear. Hmmm ... like being terrified as you're wheeled into surgery, but telling jokes anyway. Guilty. That was me.

This is all good news to those of us who fear something, as it means we also have the potential to be courageous. But why bother contemplating courage at all, both that of the human race, and, on a smaller scale, our own? Why use up valuable time and monetary resources? What does it all matter? It matters very much.

First of all, think of the ramifications of a courage-lacking society. History is full of examples, and they aren't pretty stories. Secondly, understanding what our courage is can help prepare us for when we need to use it. If the exercises that help us achieve a patient, stress-free life could also help us access our courage, then success in major events, and life in general, might be more attainable. That's as true for troops going into battle as it is for those of us struggling to pick our heads up off the pillow each morning.

Thirdly, it's important to understand that courage has often been very narrowly defined. Such judgement has done us a disservice. Courage isn't just one shade of human behavior; it's a million shades. Sometimes it's bold and very public; other times it's quiet and private. Whether or not it's witnessed by others doesn't measure its existence or importance. Furthermore, it's a quality that *everyone* can access, and all quantities count. We may be petrified to jump into a swimming pool, but that doesn't mean sticking our toes in, and then going up to our knees and then our waist, aren't huge acts of courage.

The most important reason for us to understand courage, however, and to attempt it in our lives, is what it does for those around us. We set a tangible example for them. This was never more true than when I re-read a card my granddaughter had given me the day I met my oncologist for the first time.

"Look deep down and if you believe, you will find courage, and nothing can stop you,"

she wrote in her sweet, nine-year-old script.

"Just wanted you to know that you have courage."

I was astounded. We had never had a conversation about courage. In fact, I don't remember ever uttering the word to her. Somehow, though, the message had gotten through. And while I was putting up a courageous front for her, and all the rest of my family and friends, I forgot how really frightened I was. This, in turn, must have made them think I was even more courageous, which set the bar higher for me, and caused me (ever the over-achiever) to work harder for them. Agreed, it's kind of a screwy way to suck it up and march forward, but it worked. I'm thinking it might work for others, too.

A few days before she gave me the card, I was hugging my granddaughter, and she asked me if cancer was contagious. Her question made me realize how much drama had flown past her in recent days, and how we needed to make sure she was kept up to speed, if only in kid-friendly terms. I smile now when I think of that conversation. I'm very glad cancer *isn't* contagious, as I would have missed all those hugs. I'm equally glad to have discovered courage *is* contagious, and am even more pleased that she might catch it.

# Lesson 20:

# A New Beginning

*The ultimate measure of a man is not where he stands in moments of comfort and conveniences, but where he stands at times of challenge and controversy.*
- Martin Luther King, Jr.

Finding a starting and end point for some things is easy: a ball of yarn, the days in a month, the length of a football field. Life challenges are different. Their onsets may be clear. But they are frequently so enormous and so overwhelming that even when they appear to be over, shadows of them remain, like an old stain on a white lace tablecloth.

I decided that Cancer Me would forever become a part of my past the very moment I finished my last chemotherapy infusion. That seemed like the perfect exclamation point to a pretty tough run. In retrospect, that was a little overly optimistic, even for me. I had done a great deal of research on my disease, surgery and treatment, but I had done no research on the after-effects of chemo. The lingering aches, pains and fatigue are aggravating, and I must remind myself daily to reread the lesson on patience.

With Cancer Me a memory, it's now the job of Watcher Me to wrap up that chapter of my life and start writing the next. Together, we're looking back at all that unfolded as if we were thumbing through the pages of a photo album. The changes in nature from spring to winter that occurred outside during this saga mirror the wisdom I think I gained going through it. I progressed from a spring neophyte to an autumnal wise woman.

At the risk of sounding like the proverbial Pollyanna, I really do look around me at least once a day and think how glad I am to be alive. I love the rain and the sun, the hot and the cold, summer's flowers and autumn's leaves. I am humbled by the love of my family and friends, as well as that of people I scarcely knew at the outset of this journey. I am promising myself not to fret about a few extra pounds or bad hair days that may be in my future, and I'm realistic enough to recognize that I'll forget that promise occasionally. Plus, I have the lessons in this book to review.

A new beginning shouldn't be a daunting task, but instead, an exciting event, something best launched with a short set of instructions. Think in terms of those that accompany a child's toy, the ones bearing the words: "Assembles in just minutes," because a new beginning really does:

1. Pick the exact time your new beginning will start. It could be obvious, like the end of chemo, receiving your final divorce papers, the first day of your new job. Or it could be an arbitrary date in the future, a target at which to aim. The good news is YOU are in charge of when your new beginning will start.

2. Don't think about the details of your life challenge that still linger, like that tablecloth stain I mentioned earlier. They are not the reminders of how terrible things were during your challenge.

They're your motivators: You've seen the dark
side of the mountain and you've come out on the
other side triumphant!

3.  Don't let a bad day go by without hope for a
    better tomorrow.  Lance Armstrong wrote in his
    autobiography, "If children have the ability to
    ignore all odds and percentages, then maybe we
    can learn from them. When you think about it,
    what other choice is there but to hope? We have
    two options, medically and emotionally: give up,
    or fight like hell."  Very true.

4.  Don't be discouraged if your new beginning has
    to be rescheduled, or if you have multiple new
    beginnings.  Who cares?  They're *your* new
    beginnings, you can have as many as you want.
    In fact, the more the merrier, because with each
    one, you're moving in a forward direction.

5.  Finally, and maybe most poignantly, remember to
    be grateful for having had the opportunity to
    square off against your adversity.  It's easy to look
    at those who suffer and mumble (with good
    intention), "I understand." Now you really *DO* get
    it.  And that makes you better equipped than most

> to hold out your hand and help the one on the
> ladder below you.

My new beginning put big spotlights on those three things I mentioned in the introduction of this book; the ones I believe right down to my very soul. Remember them? Allow me to tickle your memory just in case.

First, Cancer Me has definitely left the building. I can't help but think of her periodically and I understand that's not unusual when we overcome a life challenge. Equally common are the momentary flashbacks, followed by a sting of panic and the question, "What if that happens to me all over again?" The answer is that we can't control everything, so we might as well make better use of our time by taking a deep breath and rereading lessons one through nineteen on the preceeding pages.

The second belief I hold is that everything happens for a reason, even the bad things. That thought is tightly connected to the third belief: it is the responsibility of each of us to help improve the world around us. If we use our bad experiences to help us do that, then they will have been worth the struggle. If only one person learns courage, humor, patience, acceptance or any of the other really important lessons in this book, then my breast cancer wasn't a useless experience.

I realize, of course, there's lots of other stuff we all have to deal with in our lives. But it's the smaller stuff, so remember, in the end, it's just hair.

**Food for Thought:**

So you've finished reading this book. Hopefully it made you feel warm and fuzzy. But now what? How are you going to apply the information you've just soaked up?

Here's my suggestion: go to our website, www.courageconceptspublising.com/itsjusthair. Click on the *Food for Thought* link and you'll find a list of questions to ponder, alone or with others. They're free of charge with no strings attached, designed to encourage you to use these 20 Essential Life Lessons in facing your personal challenges.

Judith Pearson's writing career began in a tree: a wonderful old maple in her parents' backyard, with a perfect branch on which to sit. It was there, as a teenager, that she first wrote her thoughts on current events and life in general. Now hundreds of thousands of words later, this Michigan native is still writing.

A graduate of Michigan State University, Pearson has written nearly a hundred newspaper and magazine articles. In addition, she has published two books, both biographies about ordinary people who exhibited extraordinary courage: *Belly of the Beast: a POW's Inspiring True Story of Faith, Courage and Survival,* and *Wolves at the Door: the True Story of America's Greatest Female Spy.* The latter has been optioned for a movie.

The founder of Courage Concepts, an organization that fosters courage in women, Pearson provides workshops and keynotes for corporations and organizations. An unexpected life challenge caused her to realize what life is really all about.

Several years ago, Judy returned to her idyllic little home town on the shores of Lake Michigan, where she lives with her husband. And she still climbs trees.

Made in the USA
Charleston, SC
23 February 2012